IN THE SPACE of a single generation, Detroit managed to ruin itself. Some of the factors that led to the immolation of Detroit are unique to the city and its politics, but some are not. As the nation watches the city descend into insolvency and chaos, the question is: Is Detroit an outlier, or is it just ahead of the curve?

The proximate cause of Detroit's bankruptcy is its inability to make good on debts owed to the funds paying out pensions and health care benefits to current and retired city workers. Those obligations make up the great majority of Detroit's $20 billion or so in outstanding debt. While the city's population has been plummeting since the 1950s, its public sector has continued to grow relative to the size of its population. In 2011, it maintained nearly 13,000 city employees, or one municipal employee for every 55 residents, twice the number of larger cities such as Charlotte and Fort Worth. (That one may write "larger cities such as Charlotte and Fort Worth" speaks volumes about what has become of Detroit.) When staffing reductions have been proposed, both the unions and city officials resisted. When modest reductions were proposed in 2011, city Finance Director Tom Lijana protested, "You can't do this in one year.... I'm going to be picking up your garbage once a month. I'm only going to turn on power to your house every once in a while. You just can't do that." Yet the city of Austin, hardly a Spartan outpost of small-government skinflintery, manages to provide what are generally conceded to be very good municipal services with far fewer city employees per resident than Detroit. San Jose does so with *half* the per capita municipal workforce that Detroit maintains.

Detroit is an extreme example of the fact that public-sector employment has become in effect a supplementary welfare state, with salaries and benefits – and, above all, pensions – entirely disconnected from legitimate municipal purposes. Unionized public-sector employees with a high degree of political discipline fortified by narrow financial self-interest become an unstoppable constituency, and the government becomes its own special-interest group. But while salaries more or less have to be paid out of current revenue and therefore impose at least a measure of pain

Detroit is an extreme example of the fact that public-sector employment has become in effect a supplementary welfare state.

on taxpayers, promised future benefits need not be backed by anything more than good intentions. While there were areas in which the city proceeded responsibly – as late as 2011, its police and firefighter pension fund was being adequately provided for – many future obligations were not funded at all, or funded to only a tiny degree of the liabilities accruing. A 2012 Kennedy School study found that Detroit had set aside less than half of what it would need to fund its pensions and was attempting to fund its health-insurance and life-insurance plans on a pay-as-you-go basis, resulting in unfunded liabilities amounting to a massive $5 billion.

In spite of these growing liabilities, Detroit's public-sector workers consistently managed to increase their share of the city's workforce while stopping dead any and all efforts at meaningful reform.

They have been empowered to resist reform by a particularly nasty form of racialist politics that has reached its fullest expression in Detroit but is by no means limited to that unhappy city. When the mayor of Philadelphia boasts that "the brothers and sisters are in charge," when the mayor of Washington declares the nation's capital a "chocolate city," they are cultivating the same sort of tribalism that has helped make Detroit what it is. The tolerance for black racism in American politics

[4]

is striking. When Representative Joe Mitchell, an Alabama Democrat, was challenged by a constituent about a question related to gun rights, Mitchell responded that he was elected to represent the interests of blacks and maintained that he could care less about the interests of his white correspondent and those of his "slave-holding, murdering, adulterous, baby-raping, incestuous, snaggle-toothed, backward-assed, inbreed [*sic*], imported, criminal-minded kin folk." The anti-Semitic remarks of the Rev. Jesse Jackson and the Rev. Al Sharpton are of course well documented, as is the habit of mostly Democratic black politicians of consorting with such openly racist demagogues as Louis Farrakhan. It is an irony of our history that the political home of black racism in American politics is also the historical political home of white racism: the Democratic Party.

The end point of such politics is Detroit. As late as 1960, Detroit was the most affluent city in the United States – and perhaps the most affluent industrial city in the world –

with a per capita income exceeding that of any other U.S. city, according to the U.S. Census Bureau. In 1961, it elected as its mayor Jerome Cavanagh, a 33-year-old Democrat whose youth and idealism brought immediate and inevitable comparisons to John F. Kennedy. Cavanagh's triumph was a surprise, and he was borne to victory on the strength of an African-American vote whose power had not yet been fully appreciated. Added to the Democratic allegiances of Catholic white ethnics, the subordination of the conservative-voting auto-workers to their left-leaning union bosses, and the growing sympathy for Kennedy–Johnson-style progressivism among the professional classes, the attachment of the black vote to the Democratic cause meant the end of Republicans in Detroit and the establishment of a de facto one-party government.

The effects would prove catastrophic in a remarkably short period of time.

But Cavanagh entered office on a wave of optimism. He promised reform, and reform was needed – and seemed within reach. Already in the 1950s and early 1960s, Detroit had troubles, but they were not insurmountable. Detroit, like many similar cities, had a problem: the concentration of poverty and related social dysfunction in its inner city – in no small part a legacy of the explosion of the city's black population during the Great Migration, soaring from 6,000 in 1910 to 120,000 in 1929 and from 1.2 percent of the population in 1910 to about 30 percent of the population by the election of Cavanagh. It is one of the great tragedies of American history that wherever black Americans go, from the Jim Crow South to the great industrial cities, they are persecuted by the Democratic Party, then help entrench the power of that party.

The black workers arriving to fill industrial jobs in Detroit found discrimination very similar to what they had endured in the South, with Democratic politicians such as Representative Rudolph G. Tenerowicz leading efforts on behalf of their white-ethnic working-class constituents to prevent desegregation, especially when it came to housing. The segregation of

It is an irony of our history that the political home of black racism in American politics is also the historical political home of white racism: the Democratic Party.

housing would prove to be the flashpoint for the periods of civil unrest that give Detroit the distinction of being the only U.S. city to have been occupied by federal troops on three occasions.

Tenerowicz was among the key political figures who fought the 1943 effort of the Detroit Housing Commission – then under the leadership of Republican Mayor Edward Jeffries and his reform-minded director-secretary, 25-year-old George Clifton Edwards Jr. – to build a housing project for black defense workers in a largely Polish section of the city. The backlash against this plan resulted in, among other

[8]

dispiriting displays, the insalubrious spectacle of a mob of pale-faced Polish Americans holding up signs reading "We Want White Tenants in Our Community" in front of a housing project named after Sojourner Truth. The Rev. Charles Hill, a prominent civil-rights activist, wryly observed at the time that his opponents were under the mistaken impression that Sojourner Truth was a Polish woman.

Tenerowicz was joined in his effort by the unholy leadership of Father Constantine Dzink, whose sermons highlighted the danger of "the Jews and niggers making a combination" in local politics. (The theory that Protestant Republicans and Jews colluded to place black housing projects in Catholic areas in order to break up Democratic voting blocs is absolutely deathless, still with us in the work of the Catholic polemicist E. Michael Jones and others of his ilk.) The Ku Klux Klan was not unheard-of in Michigan, but more common were organizations such as the Fenelon-Seven Mile Road Development Association, Detroit's version of the South's white citizens' councils. Facing pressure from white Democratic constituencies, Franklin Roosevelt's Federal Housing Administration (FHA) decided that the Sojourner Truth project would be a whites-only development, while a blacks-only project would be built elsewhere – outside the city limits. After sustained protest, the FHA again reversed itself, and eventually a number of black families – who already had paid rent and signed leases in anticipation of moving into their new homes – began to relocate into the project, doing so in the face of an armed mob and by the light of a burning cross. Some 1,600 National Guard troops and 1,100 police officers had to be dispatched to prevent their being lynched.

Those racial tensions were further exacerbated when 25,000 white autoworkers at Packard walked off the job to protest the hiring of three black men to work on the assembly line. Three weeks later, Detroit erupted into a full-fledged race riot. Mayor Jeffries begged the federal government for help, which was not immediately forthcoming – not until the

Germans began using Detroit's bloodshed in their propaganda efforts. After having his advisers cook up a legal rationale that would save his having to formally declare martial law, President Roosevelt dispatched federal troops to occupy Detroit. Some 6,000 soldiers would be needed to restore peace in the city.

It was the beginning of the end of Republican power in Detroit, which had elected a good deal many more Whigs to its mayoralty than Democrats. Before Jeffries's time, the Democrats had won election to the mayor's office only five times in the 20th century, as opposed to 14 times for the Republicans. Jeffries was the fifth of five back-to-back Republican mayors preceded by the Democratic reformer Frank Murphy – who was himself preceded by five back-to-back Republican mayors. The Democrats had not won consecutive mayoralties since the 19th century.

But the riots badly damaged Jeffries's standing. His political machine kept him in power until 1948, when Democrat Eugene Van Antwerp sent him back to the city council. The

1949 election saw Jeffries's young housing director, now aligned with the Democrats, running on a civil-rights platform in a racially charged election against Republican Albert Cobo. The Republican won, but the GOP was increasingly alienated from the black vote. Cobo was succeeded by Republican Louis Miriani, a corrupt party-machine man who would later serve time in prison for tax fraud – but not before losing the election to the charismatic young Jerome Cavanagh, the first of Detroit's Democrats to figure out how to marry the black vote to the union vote. Detroit would never elect another Republican mayor, at least as of this writing.

Cavanagh's administration came out like gangbusters, and for years he could do no wrong as far as Democrats were concerned – which now meant, as a practical matter, as far as political Detroit was concerned. Having run as a civil-rights man, he marched in the streets of Detroit with the Rev. Martin Luther King Jr. and 100,000 constituents. He appointed a reform-minded police chief and instituted affirmative-action programs. He proved to be an expert at wringing money out of the federal government. President Lyndon Johnson was an admirer and an ally, and his Model Cities Program showered money on Detroit – and made Mayor Cavanagh the only sitting elected official to serve on its board. The riots of 1943, all the well-informed people said, were a distant memory. We were to have a Great Society, with Detroit as its model city. For a time, it seemed likely that the progressive vision of urban renewal under an expert technocratic administration would be realized. The *National Observer* wrote during Cavanagh's first term:

The evidence, both statistical and visual, is everywhere. Retail sales are up dramatically. Earnings are higher. Unemployment is lower. People are putting new aluminum sidings on their homes, new carpets on the floor, new cars in the garage.

Some people are forsaking the suburbs and returning to the city. Physically Detroit has acquired freshness and vitality. Acres of slums have been razed, and steel and glass apartments, angular and lonely in the vacated landscape, have sprung up in their place. In the central business district, hard by the Detroit River, severely rectangular skyscrapers – none more than 5 years old – jostle uncomfortably with the gilded behemoths of another age.

Accustomed to years of adversity, to decades of drabness and civil immobility, Detroiters are naturally exhilarated. They note with particular pride that Detroit has been removed from the Federal Bureau of Employment Security's classification of "an area with substantial and persistent unemployment."

But there was a problem. In 1962, the city had faced a serious fiscal deficit – $28 million, back when that meant something – but the young mayor was not about to back away from his ambitious agenda. That meant more money, and that meant new taxes and higher taxes. Among them were a city income tax and a city commuter tax, which Cavanagh was empowered to establish after a fight with the state legislature. Armed with his new revenue-reaping

> *Ironically, it was Detroit's signature product – the automobile – that hastened the city's dissolution.*

tools, Cavanagh set about building his urban utopia, and he made the same unpleasant discovery that has, slowly and painfully, dawned upon central planners, reformers, and utopians of all stripes over the ages: nobody wanted to live in his model city.

Contrary to the *National Observer*'s observations, Detroit's population had peaked in the 1950 census. It soon was losing more than 20,000 residents a year on net. But that does not begin to tell the whole story. From 1960 to 1970, Detroit lost 158,662 people on net – some 22,000 in 1966 alone. But it lost nearly twice that many white residents: 344,093 of them from 1960 to 1970. In 1950, there were 1.5 million whites living in Detroit, virtually all of whom – all but 75,000 – would leave by 2010. Throughout the 1960s and beyond, the combination of higher taxes, crime, civil disorder (especially the 1967 riots), and the declining quality of schools and other government institutions created enormous pressure for people and businesses to relocate outside the city limits. The new plants serving the increasingly decentralized automobile industry moved outside the city, and the workers – also the taxpayers – followed them. The white residents, being generally better off and more able to secure jobs and housing elsewhere, led the way.

Ironically, it was Detroit's signature product – the automobile – that hastened the city's dissolution. Under the leadership of President Dwight D. Eisenhower, the United States had begun in the postwar period the country's greatest experiment with economic central planning: the federal highway system. Cities such as New York and Boston (and, to a lesser extent, Philadelphia) had geographic and social forces that helped preserve their urban cores, whereas truly postwar cities such as Houston were simply organized around the automobile and incorporated outlying areas as the population shifted. Detroit, like many Rust Belt cities, had neither factor to reinforce its municipal integrity. While sprawling, automobile-centric Los Angeles saw its population double from 1940 to 1980, despite the decline of key industries such as furniture making and steel, Detroit continued to trickle away. The federal government paved the way to the suburbs, and the city of Detroit gave its people ever more powerful incentives to take those roads and never look back.

Like the rest of the country, Detroit missed a critical opportunity in the immediate postwar era. The United States was in an unprecedented position: it was the sole surviving major industrial power that had not been ravaged by the war. In the immediate postwar era, the United States was home to at least half – and possibly more – of the world's manufacturing capacity, a not insignificant chunk of it in Detroit. And those factories were humming. The United States was producing 60 percent of the entire world's manufacturing output. The nation alone constituted 61 percent of the total economic output of the countries that now make up the OECD. The Eisenhower administration had success wringing the postwar inflation out of the economy with a conservative monetary policy, which contributed to a series of small recessions that had little effect on employment or wages, which were robust, especially as wartime wage and price controls were rescinded. Detroit's working men enjoyed undreamed-of prosperity, and the city had a thriving black middle class. It is disheartening to consider the counterfactual case of what the United States and its industrial capital might have done had our political and economic leadership fully appreciated the uniqueness of our economic position and, most important, the inescapably transitory nature of that position. Instead, we set about building the welfare state. Government grew at all levels, and unions in the private sector − notably Detroit's autoworkers – set about creating unsustainable workplace practices and compensation structures that would eventually put them out of jobs, while their counterparts in the public sector set about looting the fiscs. The model of government at the federal, state, and local

---

The model of government at the federal, state, and local level that emerged in the late 1950s and 1960s was built on a defective foundation: the belief that the postwar economic boom would last forever.

---

level that emerged in the late 1950s and 1960s was built on a defective foundation: the belief that the postwar economic boom would last forever. While Vietnam and desegregation were the headline issues of the 1960s, much of the real domestic politics of the period consisted of infighting over the money from the postwar economic boom, with little or no attention given to the fact that the money would someday run out.

And it has run out spectacularly in Detroit.

The textbook example of postwar short-sightedness was the debacle of Cavanagh's attempt to implement the Model Cities program. The Johnson administration was generous with the money, but Detroit was divided over what to do with it. Local business interests – back when Detroit had local business interests – wanted the money to be invested in the downtown commercial district, creating an urban anchor for the city, but they gave little thought to the question of who, exactly, would inhabit the skyscrapers they envisioned at a time when the city's population was in steep decline. The Detroit left – the community organizers, if you will – wanted the money to be invested in housing projects and other affordable-housing developments, along with the usual array of antipoverty programs, the unstated purpose of which is to provide comfortable employment for the politically connected. As in other Model Cities such as Newark, Camden, and Atlanta, Detroit's efforts to shore up its city center went up in flames with the riots of the 1960s.

The 1967 Detroit race riot was the largest civil disturbance since the Civil War and the New York City draft riots. Some 2,000 buildings were burned to the ground; 7,200 people were arrested; 1,189 injured; and 43 left dead – killed by snipers, beaten by mobs, immolated alive in burning buildings. Firefighters were gunned down while trying to put out the flames of the city. Cavanagh, a Democrat, hesitated to seek assistance from Governor George Romney, while President Johnson hesitated to deploy troops at the request of Governor Romney, who was expected to be his opponent in the 1968 presidential election. As the politics were sorted out, the city burned. Eventually, Johnson invoked the Insurrection Act of 1807 and deployed 4,700

> *Detroit is a city in which black identity politics has trumped, and continues to trump, every other consideration, from basic finances to public safety.*

troops from the 82nd Airborne, while Romney sent in the National Guard. *Newsweek* described the aftermath:

> *The trouble burst on Detroit like a firestorm and turned the nation's fifth biggest city into a theater of war. Whole streets lay ravaged by looters, whole blocks immolated by flames. Federal troops – the first sent into racial battle outside the South in a quarter of a century – occupied American streets at bayonet point. Patton tanks – machine guns ablaze – and Huey helicopters patrolled a cityscape of blackened brick chimneys poking out of gutted basements. And suddenly Harlem 1964*

*and Watts 1965 and Newark only three weeks
ago fell into the shadows of memory. Detroit was
the new benchmark, its rubble a monument to
the most devastating race riot in U.S. history –
and a symbol of domestic crisis grown graver
than any since the Civil War.*

It is worth noting that while Detroit already was in decline in the 1960s, the position of its black middle class was very strong. As the economist Thomas Sowell notes, "Before the ghetto riot of 1967, Detroit's black population had the highest rate of home-ownership of any black urban population in the country, and their unemployment rate was just 3.4 percent. It was not despair that fueled the riot."

What was it?

Mohandas K. Gandhi famously told representatives of the British Raj that India, like any self-respecting country, would prefer bad government under its own people to good government under a foreign power. A similar notion has held sway in Detroit, but its motivating factor is racism rather than nationalism.

Detroit is a city in which black identity politics has trumped, and continues to trump, every other consideration, from basic finances to public safety. In 1974, Detroit's racial politics would come to full fruition with the election of Mayor Coleman Young, an incompetent administrator, a friend of corruption – two of his closest political allies, who happened to be serving as police chief and deputy police chief, managed to loot $2.6 million from city funds between the two of them – and a practitioner of poisonous racial politics who nonetheless managed to keep himself in the mayor's office for 20 years, thereby foreclosing any opportunity the city might have had to reverse its course. As James Q. Wilson put it, "Mayor Coleman Young rejected the integrationist goal in favor of a flamboyant, black-power style that won him loyal followers, but he left the city a fiscal and social wreck." Young's stock-in-trade was blaming whites for the problems of an increasingly whites-free city, charging that, in his words, "the money was carried out in the pockets of the businesses and the white people."

As Nolan Finley notes in the *Detroit News*, Mayor Young's spirit is very much alive in "the black nationalism that is now the dominant ideology of the council." Finley reported on the city council's debate regarding the expansion of a city convention center. Many of those backing the project, and many of the union members who would be employed to work on it, were white, which infuriated both the council members and the residents who showed up to denounce the project. The assembled crowd shouted that whites addressing the issue should "go home," while council president Monica Conyers dismissed the case of a white union representative with these words: "Those workers look like you – they don't look like me." But race was not Conyers's sole concern in matters of municipal finance: she was subsequently convicted on bribery charges related to city contracts. Other members of the city council have proposed the creation of blacks-only city contracts and a blacks-only enterprise zone. The city has considered restricting some grant money to black-owned businesses under the rubric of "minority" economic development – in a city that is 80 percent black.

From Cavanagh to Young to the current dispute over the city's bankruptcy, the combination of racial politics and union financial interests has undermined every public institution in Detroit. And while the black-power style may be the most remarkable feature of Detroit's poisonous political coalition, the unions have the upper hand. As life for blacks – and everybody else – in Detroit deteriorated, the ever more deeply entrenched unions installed political candidates who rewarded them with ever more extravagant promises of compensation, benefits, and retirement pensions. That the city was in no way positioned to make good on those benefits apparently mattered little to Detroit's ruling class, which has been happy to trade promises of future payouts in exchange for immediate power and financial rewards. Their actions have ranged from the negligent to the outright criminal. Mayor Kwame Kilpatrick resigned after being convicted of felony perjury and obstruction of justice. In 2010, he was returned to prison for violating his parole, and in 2013, he was convicted of 24 additional felonies ranging from extortion to bribery and fraud.

Against that background, Detroit's decision to seek protection in bankruptcy court is almost anticlimactic. Union power ensured the growth of the public sector; racial hostility and municipal incompetence drove first the white middle class and then the black middle class out of the city and ensured that as Detroit's signature industry struggled, no

The main interest of the sorry case of Detroit is to learn how long it takes to entirely ruin a prosperous city.

new centers of economic activity emerged to replace it. It had always been a matter of time – indeed, the main interest of the sorry case of Detroit is to learn how long it takes to entirely ruin a prosperous city. The answer is less than one generation in the worst-case scenario, but possibly longer for cities that suffer the same kind of problems as Detroit to a lesser degree.

Detroit's decline is related to the decline of the automobile industry but was not an inevitable outcome of it. Many cities have seen their key industries shrink or evaporate without descending into similar chaos. But the autoworkers' unions bear a special responsibility for Detroit's cultural and economic troubles inasmuch as they undermined their industry and the institutions related to it at the very moment Detroit most needed them. In addition to simply being greedy, they were also caught up in the same countercultural nihilism as the rest of the country in the 1960s and 1970s. John Lippert, who worked to build Cadillacs at the Fleetwood plant during those years, tells the story: "Our militancy at GM drew on the youthful rebellion that was gripping the U.S. Hundreds of us at Fleetwood, black and white, grew our hair long, fueled by antiestablishment fervor that helped end the Vietnam War and sweep Richard Nixon out of the White House. During our 30-minute lunch breaks, we sat in our cars and listened to Jimi Hendrix as we smoked marijuana, drank beer, and took Desoxyn and other methamphetamines before returning to the line. Our quality levels and absenteeism rates were among GM's worst. We didn't care."

GM's bailout by the federal government was an exercise in lawlessness, but at least this much can be said for it: GM produces actual goods. It has assets, products, facilities, and production capacity. Detroit already is sniffing around for a federal bailout, too, but there is, practically speaking, nothing to save. One-third of the city's land is vacant or derelict. Half its streetlights have been rendered inoperable by thieves stripping the copper wiring. It has more than 120,000 vacant homes and empty lots. It is closing its schools and police stations and discontinuing some public transport, in part because it cannot afford to operate the buses and in part because their drivers are too afraid to drive them on the city's lawless streets. Its notional unemployment rate was 16 percent in April 2013; its real unemployment rate is probably closer to 50 percent. Its murder rate is about 11 times that of New York City. The median value of a home in the city is $9,000. When the Cold War classic *Red Dawn* was remade in 2012, the producers saved themselves some of the cost of creating a postapocalyptic United States by filming in Detroit, though filming had to be stopped when councilwoman JoAnn Watson, in a car with municipal plates, parked in the middle of a scene and refused to leave.

Detroit has at least $20 billion in debts that it cannot pay. Its unfunded liabilities related to union pensions and benefits may prove greater still. The bankruptcy is playing out according to Detroit rules, which means a combination of racialist politics and union self-dealing. Rick Snyder, the Republican governor of Michigan, was denounced as a racist for appointing an emergency financial manager to oversee the city's insolvency. The manager, Kevyn Orr, is a black man who was denounced as an "Uncle Tom" by the Rev. Charles Williams II, the head of the Michigan division of the Rev. Al Sharpton's National Action Network. A crowd marched on the governor's private residence, chanting, "Detroit won't go to the back of the bus. No EFMs. No racist cuts." The unions, which are threatened with losing pension payments worth billions of dollars, challenged in court the city's very legal right to seek bankruptcy protection, though federal law explicitly provides for it, and a local judge attempted to throw the bankruptcy out unilaterally, much to the amusement of the federal courts, which have jurisdiction in the matter. Detroit has, at this counting, more than 100,000 creditors making claims against its empty purse. Simply cataloging those claims and beginning the process of adjudicating them may take years.

Mayor Young, of all people, was insightful

about the effects of the riot and its aftermath. "Detroit's losses went a hell of a lot deeper than the immediate toll of lives and buildings," he wrote in his autobiography. "The

The bankruptcy is playing out according to Detroit rules, which means a combination of racialist politics and union self-dealing.

riot put Detroit on the fast track to economic desolation, mugging the city and making off with incalculable value in jobs, earnings taxes, corporate taxes, retail dollars, sales taxes, mortgages, interest, property taxes, development dollars, investment dollars, tourism dollars, and plain damn money."

Detroit is not alone in its situation. Other cities — and large states such as California — face similar problems. It is worth noting that

Detroit's heavy pension liabilities, amounting to about $19,000 per household, still are only the fifth worst in the country, according to the Kennedy School study, with Chicago leading the way and New York City, San Francisco, and Boston in worse shape than Detroit. The difference is that none of those other cities, even Chicago, is an obvious economic basket case. Indeed, San Francisco and New York are the centers of two of the nation's most productive economic sectors: technology and finance. A highly productive economy can carry the weight of a lot of political misdeeds before it collapses under the burden.

But there are limits. Detroit is a case of the parasite having outgrown the host. Whether that will be the case in cities such as San Francisco or in states such as California remains to be seen. Indeed, the main challenge for reformers at the state and local – and national – level for the coming generation is: Don't become Detroit. But reform is neither politically easy nor necessarily popular.

And if the Age of Obama has taught us any-thing, it is that shouting "Racist!" while loot-ing the treasury is a viable political strategy beyond Detroit.

Copyright © 2013 by Kevin D. Williamson

All rights reserved. No part of this publication may be reproduced, stored in a retrieval system, or transmitted, in any form or by any means, electronic, mechanical, photocopying, recording, or otherwise, without the prior written permission of Encounter Books, 900 Broadway, Suite 601, New York, New York, 10003.

First American edition published in 2013 by Encounter Books, an activity of Encounter for Culture and Education, Inc., a nonprofit, tax exempt corporation.
Encounter Books website address: www.encounterbooks.com

Manufactured in the United States and printed on acid-free paper. The paper used in this publication meets the minimum requirements of ANSI/NISO Z39.48–1992 (R 1997) (*Permanence of Paper*).

FIRST AMERICAN EDITION

LIBRARY OF CONGRESS
CATALOGING-IN-PUBLICATION DATA IS AVAILABLE

ISBN10: 1-59403-746-9
ISBN13: 978-1-59403-746-7
E-BOOK: 978-1-59403-747-4

10 9 8 7 6 5 4 3 2 1

SERIES DESIGN BY CARL W. SCARBROUGH